Dinosaurs

Compsognathus

by Julie Murray

1

Dash!
LEVELED READERS
An Imprint of Abdo Zoom • abdobooks.com

Dash!
LEVELED READERS

1

Level 1 – Beginning
Short and simple sentences with familiar words or patterns for children who are beginning to understand how letters and sounds go together.

Level 2 – Emerging
Longer words and sentences with more complex language patterns for readers who are practicing common words and letter sounds.

Level 3 – Transitional
More developed language and vocabulary for readers who are becoming more independent.

THIS BOOK CONTAINS RECYCLED MATERIALS

abdobooks.com

Published by Abdo Zoom, a division of ABDO, PO Box 398166, Minneapolis, Minnesota 55439.

Printed in the United States of America, North Mankato, Minnesota.
052024
092024

Photo Credits: Alamy, Science Source, Shutterstock
Production Contributors: Kenny Abdo, Jennie Forsberg, Grace Hansen, John Hansen
Design Contributors: Neil Klinepier

Library of Congress Control Number: 2023948550

Publisher's Cataloging in Publication Data

Names: Murray, Julie, author.
Title: Compsognathus / by Julie Murray
Description: Minneapolis, Minnesota : Abdo Zoom, 2025 | Series: Dinosaurs | Includes online resources and index.
Identifiers: ISBN 9781098285432 (lib. bdg.) | ISBN 9781098286132 (ebook) | ISBN 9781098286484 (Read-to-me eBook)
Subjects: LCSH: Dinosaurs--Juvenile literature. | Compsognathus--Juvenile literature. | Prehistoric animals--Juvenile literature. | Paleontology--Juvenile literature. | Extinct animals--Juvenile literature.
Classification: DDC 567.9--dc23

Table of Contents

Compsognathus

Compsognathus (komp-sog-nay-thus) was a **theropod** dinosaur. It lived 150 million years ago.

It lived near coastal areas in what is Europe today.

It is one of the smallest known dinosaurs. It was the size of a chicken.

Its body was two feet (0.6 m) long. It weighed just seven pounds (3 kg).

Compsognathus walked on two long legs. It had two short arms.

Its tail was long. This helped with balance.

Compsognathus had a pointed head. Its teeth were small and sharp.

It was an **agile** hunter. It ate small animals, such as lizards and insects.

The first Compsognathus **fossils** were discovered in 1858. They were found in Bavaria, Germany.

More Facts

- *Compsognathus* means "elegant jaw." It is named for the small bones in its head.
- The dinosaur was built for speed. It could run 40 miles per hour (64.4 kph)!
- Scientists think the dinosaur may have had short **bristles** that covered its body.

Glossary

agile – moving quickly and gracefully.

bristle – a short, stiff hair on an animal.

fossil – the remains or trace of a living animal or plant from a long time ago. Fossils are found embedded in earth or rock.

theropod – any dinosaur of the suborder Theropoda, such as Tyrannosaurus rex and velociraptor, characterized by hollow bones and three-toed limbs, usually possessing short forelimbs and walking on two legs.

Index

Online Resources

Booklinks
NONFICTION NETWORK
FREE! ONLINE NONFICTION RESOURCES

To learn more about Compsognathus, please visit **abdobooklinks.com** or scan this QR code. These links are routinely monitored and updated to provide the most current information available.